Creative Matting and Framing

for Photos, Artwork, and Collections

Creative Matting and Framing

for Photos, Artwork, and Collections

BY TRICE BOERENS

PHOTOGRAPHY BY
KEVIN DILLEY

WATSON-GUPTILL PUBLICATIONS / NEW YORK

Trice Boerens is an award-winning product designer, art director, and author who has worked on over 200 books on quilting, dollmaking, painting, beadweaving, and a variety of other crafts subjects. She lives in Ogden, Utah.

Kevin Dilley is a commercial photographer whose company, Propix Imaging, is located in Riverdale, Utah.

SENIOR EDITOR: Joy Aquilino
EDITOR: Amy Handy
DESIGN: pink design, inc. (www.pinkdesigninc.com)
GRAPHIC PRODUCTION: Hector Campbell
PHOTOGRAPHY: Kevin Dilley
PRINCIPAL TEXT TYPE: Mrs. Eaves Roman

Copyright © 2003 by Trice Boerens

First published in 2003 by Watson-Guptill Publications,
a division of VNU Business Media, Inc.,
770 Broadway, New York, N.Y. 10003
www.watsonguptill.com

DESIGN NOTES
The sticker designs featured in the projects on pages 38–39 and 46–47 are copyright © Punch Studio, Culver City, California 90231 / The Gifted Line / From The John Grossman Collection of Antique Images.
The greeting card featured in the project on pages 38–39 appears courtesy of Meri Meri, San Mateo, California.
The Morning Glory Engraving and Rose Leaves stamps featured in the projects on pages 51–53 and 64–65 are used by permission of Rubber Stampede, 2550 Pellissier Place, Whittier CA 90601.

LIBRARY OF CONGRESS CATALOGING-IN-PUBLICATION DATA
Boerens, Trice.
Creative matting and framing / by Trice Boerens; photography by Kevin Dilley
         p. cm.
      Includes index.
      ISBN 0-8230-1086-4 (pbk.)
1. Photographs—Trimming, mounting, etc.   2. Art—Matting.   3. Picture frames and framing.
4. Decoration and ornament.   5. Handicraft.   I. Title
      TR340 .B64 2003
      749'.7—dc21   2002013296
                                               CIP

Manufactured in Italy

First printing, 2002

1 2 3 4 5 6 7 8 9 / 10 09 08 07 06 05 04 03 02

Dedicated to my mother, Catherine,
who always looks on the bright side.

Acknowledgments

Thank you to Joy Aquilino, Amy Handy, and Margo Mooney. Also thank you to Ann Gladwell for having a picture-perfect house.

Contents

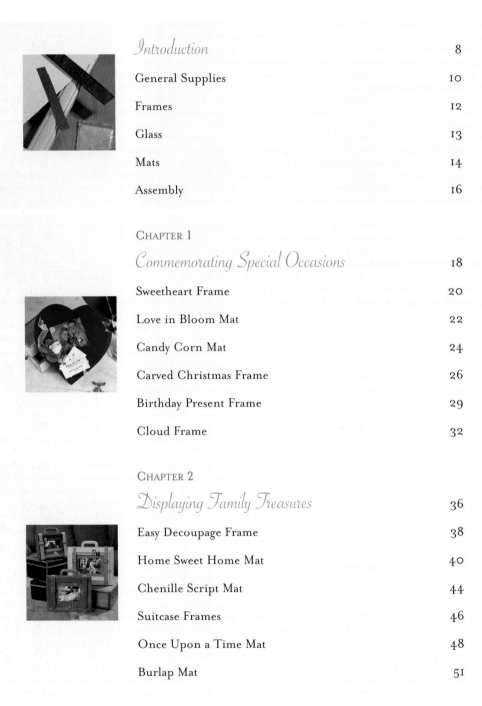

Introduction

Nowadays, both our living spaces and our work spaces have become much more personalized. To celebrate what's most important in our lives, we display portraits of those we love, landscapes of our favorite places, and mementos of special occasions. Yet simply sticking a picture in a store-bought frame is a rather impersonal way to showcase these treasures. With the interest in scrapbooking at an all-time high, many of us are looking for creative ways to bring cherished photos and other memorabilia out of the memory albums and into our homes.

This book will show you many ways to embellish various styles of mats and frames to give a unique look to your photos, collectibles, needlework, kids's artwork, and other items. This book will *not* teach you how to construct a frame from scratch, a process that requires specialized skills and expensive tools and materials. But with the wealth of attractive, inexpensive manufactured frames available today, the possibilities for transforming these purchased frames into works of art are limited only by your imagination.

Scrapbooking appeals to those of us who have a desire to preserve personal histories in a creative way. The process of assembling pages has evolved over the past several years from simple two-dimensional page layouts to elaborate three-dimensional mixed-media presentations. Many traditional crafting techniques such as beading, stitching, and wire sculpting have been cleverly incorporated into scrapbooking. This phenomenon has brought millions of new customers into craft and paper stores.

In this book we are coming full circle by adapting these "new" techniques for decorating scrapbook pages into creative methods for embellishing frames.

After you have mastered the techniques presented in this book, try using them in other applications. The dipping technique used on the Spun Gold Mats (pages 98–99) can also be used to treat fabric for making coordinating throw pillows or even curtains. Try the distressing method seen on the Distressed Frames (pages 96–97) to age wooden candlesticks or finials. Or jazz up plain boxes with stickers (pages 38–39), beach finds (pages 56–57), or decorative moss and bark (pages 62–63). Remember when adding accents to your home that change is good. Most of us stop noticing surroundings that never change, so it helps to mix things up before they become invisible to you. And what better way to transform our rooms than with creative projects we've made ourselves that celebrate the people and things we love most?

General Supplies

Nearly all the supplies needed for these projects are available in craft stores. Many projects call for such basics as tracing paper, a metal ruler, straight pins, sandpaper, paintbrushes, and foamboard, so it is best to have these on hand. Occasionally you will need a sewing machine (or a hand-sewing needle if you're willing to stitch by hand) and an iron and ironing board. Some common materials—such as craft paint, ribbons, embroidery floss, card stock, or stamp pads—will need to be purchased in specific colors to coordinate with a particular project. A trip through your favorite craft store will offer many ideas on other items to use for adorning frames.

Several projects also require sealer and/or varnish. Sealer provides a top coat that protects against moisture, dirt, and dust. It is sold as a liquid or as a spray. Varnish adds a layer of protection, and also enhances the color and detail of the surface decoration. Varnish is available in a variety of finishes: matte, satin, and gloss. Like sealer, it comes in liquid or spray form. When spraying any type of product, be sure to work in a well-ventilated area, wear safety goggles, and protect your work surface with a drop cloth or newspapers.

Cutting Tools

A mat knife is essential for cutting mats, and a sharp blade is necessary for clean cuts, so change the knife blade often. A self-healing rubber mat allows you to put pressure on the knife without bending or breaking the blade, or marring the cutting surface. A mat knife, craft knife, or X-Acto knife is needed for many other cutting chores in the projects, and scissors are also called for at times.

Adhesives

Many glues and tapes cause damage over time, so choose adhesives labeled archival or photo-safe. White craft glue works well on nonporous surfaces; hot glue is good for porous surfaces. Because masking tape loses adhesion over time and often leaves behind a sticky residue, use it only for temporary applications, such as until glue dries. Painter's tape is ideal for masking off areas when painting; it peels off easily without damaging the underlying surface.

Double-sided adhesive is sold in sheets as well as in rolls of tape $1/4$-, $1/2$-, or 1-inch-wide. Not to be confused with double-sided cellophane tape, this product is not only acid free, it is also strong enough to hold glitter, beads, or fabric. It provides a strong, instant bond that is also useful when adding three-dimensional embellishments to wood, glass, metal, or plastic.

Foam adhesive spacers are $3/8$-inch-diameter circles or squares with adhesive on both sides, available in precut sheets of various thicknesses. The projects in this book require $1/4$-inch-thick spacers.

Spray adhesive is a translucent, fast-drying aerosol glue that provides a strong and instant bond. It works well when wrapping paper around convex or concave surfaces. Be sure to work in a well-ventilated area, wear safety goggles, and protect your work surface with a drop cloth or newspapers.

Mosaic adhesive bonds glass and ceramic tiles to wood, metal, plastic, or masonry. It is packaged in squeeze bottles with applicator tips, or in plastic tubs or metal cans. When working from a can or tub, use an applicator such as a wooden popsicle stick. Read the directions and allow for adequate drying time.

Specialty Materials

A few of the projects call for either mini and micro beads, or polymer clay, all readily available in craft stores. Mini beads have a small hole for stitching but can also be glued. The much smaller micro beads are attached only with adhesive and thus have no holes.

Polymer clay is easily worked and is cured in a low-temperature household oven. Because of this, any frames it is used to cover must be heat-safe and contain no plastic parts. Sold in a rainbow of colors, polymer clay must first be conditioned by kneading in the hands. To create flat sheets of clay, you will need an acrylic clay roller or rolling pin. Polymer clay blades, which are sold in craft stores, make good clean cuts in the clay without distorting the shape or the color blend. When working with polymer clay, be sure that your work surface is flat and free of texture. A marble tile, sheet of Plexiglas, or glass cutting board works well. Do not work directly on wood finishes because the clay could damage them. Any cooking utensils that have been used with the clay, such as spoons or baking sheets, should never be used to prepare food.

Frames

Frames are sold everywhere from supermarkets to gift stores, craft shops to home improvement centers. Also hunt for frames with potential at flea markets, second-hand stores, yard sales, and even your own attic. With photocopy machines, digital printers, and software such as Kodak's Picture Maker, it is now easy to reconfigure photos. Instead of buying a costly frame to fit the photo, you can now tailor a photo fit the frame.

When choosing the right frame for your photo or artwork, keep in mind basic design principles such as scale, contrast, and balance. Make sure that there is enough visual space around the central image. It shouldn't appear to be squeezed by the mat or frame. The themes should coordinate, such as a placing a photo illustration of a barn in a frame made from barn wood. Most important, keep in mind that the frame, though important, is really secondary; the main focus should be the photo or the artwork itself.

If embellishments are to be added onto the frame, sometimes a wider frame with more surface area may be required; see, for instance, the Broken Dishes Frame (pages 102–3). In many other cases you will be adorning the mat rather than the frame, so a narrower frame should work fine.

Sometimes a frame need not even be a traditional square or rectangle of metal or wood. Sculptors often incorporate unexpected material into their compositions such as doorknobs or tableware as "found object" art. My favorite frame projects are those that are fashioned from found objects, including the Sweetheart Frame (pages 20–21), the Birthday Present Frame (pages 29–31), and the Tennis Racket Frame (pages 72–73). Keep your eyes open for items you can turn into frames, such as serving trays or window casings.

The dimensions of the finished projects are specified in the materials lists (for example, "Model measures 11 x 11 inches."). If you choose a frame or mat of a different size, be sure to adjust other measurements accordingly.

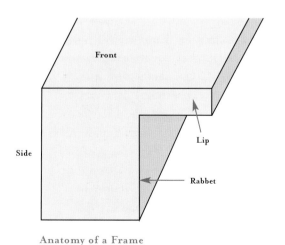

Anatomy of a Frame

Glass

Glass is usually included with purchased frames. If the frame you choose does not have glass, check craft or home improvement stores for standard-size pieces. For a relatively inexpensive option, you can have a professional glazier cut your glass. If you want to cut the glass yourself, follow the instructions below. Remember that it is always a good idea to wear safety glasses when working with glass. Some people also like to wear work gloves when cutting glass.

Please note that glass was omitted from the project photos because the lights required to photograph the finished projects would have caused glaring or hot spots when reflected off glass. (The one exception is the Sun Catcher Frame, pages 66–69, which relies on glass for its structure.) In order to use glass with the three-dimensional mats, such as the Chenille Script Mat (pages 44–45) or the Bead-Embellished Mat (pages 74–75), you may change the layering sequence when assembling and place the glass beneath the mat. If you would prefer to feature the glass on top of the mat, you may include spacers between the glass and the mat when assembling the project. (For more information, see Assembly, pages 16–17.)

Cutting Glass

1. Put on the safety glasses. Pad the work surface with an old towel or a carpet scrap. Place the glass on the padded surface. With a ruler and marker, measure and mark the glass at the point to be cut.

2. Place the straightedge along the glass, aligned with the marked spots. Hold the glass cutter at about a 90-degree angle between your index and middle fingers. Press firmly along the straightedge to score the glass with one continuous stroke. Keep in mind that a glass cutter does not actually cut through glass, but creates a fissure along which the glass will split.

3. Holding the glass firmly close to the scored line, use the pliers to break the glass along the fissure line.

4. Remove the pen marks with glass cleaner and a soft cloth.

Materials

Safety glasses
Work gloves (optional)
Old towel or carpet scrap
Glass
Metal ruler or straightedge
Carbide-tipped glass cutter
Square-jawed glazier's pliers
Fine-tip felt marker
Glass cleaner and soft cloth

Mats

Like glass, mats are often included with purchased frames. However, many of the mats shown in the projects are not standard sizes. A professional framer can cut your custom mat. Framers usually have a much wider selection of mat board colors and can add decorative beveled cuts, which are hard to reproduce without professional mat-cutting equipment. To cut your own mat, follow the instructions opposite.

Matting is the term used when artwork or photos are placed behind cut mat board, with the featured area showing through the mat window. Mounting is the term used when artwork or photos are cropped to a desired size and placed on top of the mat board, with no window.

Matting Versus Mounting

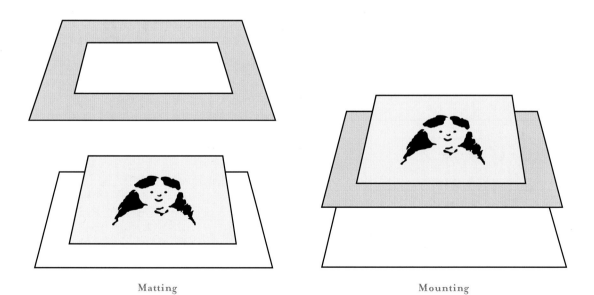

Matting   Mounting

Cutting Mats

To avoid marking the front of the mat, some framers prefer to mark the back and cut from back to front. This may result in a ragged edge on the front due to pressure from the knife. If you choose this method, remember to angle the knife in the opposite direction for the bevel.

Materials

Mat board
Pencil
Self-healing rubber mat
Metal ruler or straightedge
Craft knife or mat knife
Kneaded rubber eraser (optional)
Emery board (optional)

1. Measure and mark the mat board according to the project's diagram, or adjust the measurements if your frame is a different size or shape. (See **Photo 1**.)

2. Place the mat board on the cutting surface. Position the straightedge along the cutting line and place the knife at the top, next to the straightedge. (See **Photo 2**.)

3. Holding the straightedge securely in place, firmly draw the knife from top to bottom of the marked line in one continuous stroke. Do not go past the marked corner of the window. Lift the knife and repeat until the board is cut completely through. (It's not possible to do this in one pass.) Rotate the mat and cut the other three sides. (Note: For a beveled edge, hold the knife at a 45-degree angle.)

4. Erase visible pencil lines. If the corners are not completely precise, carefully trim them with the knife or sand lightly with an emery board. (See **Photo 3**.)

Cutting a Mat

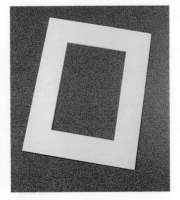

1   2   3

Assembly

To complete the framing process, layer the component parts in the desired order. (See **Diagrams 1, 2, 5, and 6.**) Secure the backing board to the frame with brown gummed tape if it is flush with the frame back, or with small nails if it is recessed into the frame back. (See **Diagrams 3 and 4.**)

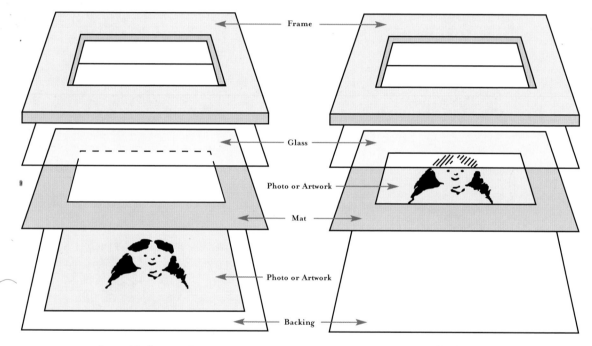

Frame

Glass

Photo or Artwork

Mat

Photo or Artwork

Backing

1. Assembly for matting

2. Assembly for mounting

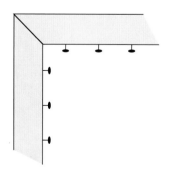

3. Assembly: Backing
secured with nails

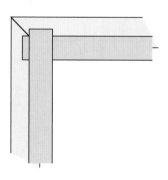

4. Assembly: Backing secured
with gummed tape

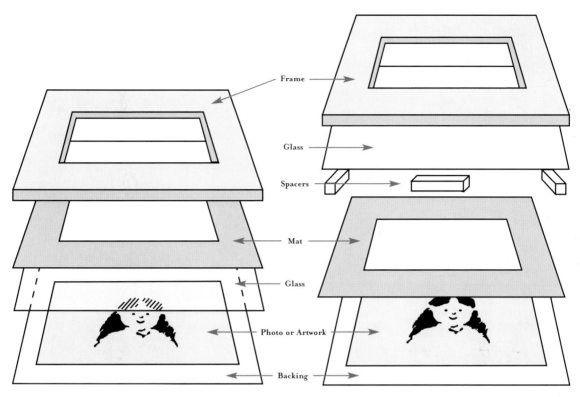

Frame

Glass

Spacers

Mat

Glass

Photo or Artwork

Backing

5. Assembly with mat on top of glass

6. Assembly with dimensional spacers

A Note on the Patterns

All patterns can be copied for private use on a commercial photocopier. The ones marked "full size" can be copied at 100 percent; others are labeled with an enlargement percentage to which the copier should be set. If your project will be a different size from the model, you may need to enlarge or reduce the patterns. Begin by determining the percentage of size difference. For example, if the actual-size pattern is for a model that is 10 inches square but your frame is 12 inches, the difference is 120 percent, so you would need to photocopy the pattern at 120 percent.

To use transfer paper, copy or trace the pattern on tracing paper. Place the transfer paper graphite side down on the project surface. Place the copied pattern right side up over the transfer paper. Lightly trace over the pattern, pressing only firmly enough to transfer the design. To make your own transfer paper, use the flat side of a number two pencil to rub a solid area of graphite on a piece of scrap or tracing paper and use this paper as you would transfer paper. Or turn the traced pattern to the wrong side and rub over the traced areas. (Be sure to place scrap paper beneath your pattern for this.)

Commemorating
Special Occasions

By design, most of life's moments are comfortable and ordinary. Sprinkled in are the milestones of birthdays and weddings, and the excitement of holidays. Honor these occasions by displaying special photos in special frames, or spread the joy by creating commemorative gifts for family and friends. All of the projects are artful combinations of color and pattern that will punctuate a remarkable day with an exclamation mark.

Sweetheart Frame

Candy boxes are a perfect found object for crafting: they are color-ful, fuzzy, and often heart-shaped. When one of my favorite six-teen-year-olds and I decided that we needed a unique way to remember her prom, the mementos came out of the box to be artfully arranged on top of it. This frame makes an ideal gift for Valentine's Day or a wedding anniversary; store love letters or romantic trinkets inside.

1. Remove the lid from the box.

2. On the inside of the lid, mark a rectangle for the window, which should be $\frac{1}{4}$ inch less all around than your photo. With a craft knife, carefully cut through the paper layer inside the lid. IMPORTANT: Do not cut through the fabric covering.

3. With scissors, cut an opening in the fabric slightly smaller than the first window. Cut diagonals in the fabric to the window corners. (See Diagram 1.)

4. Wrap the fabric to the back of the lid and glue in place. Pin the edges of the fabric in place until the glue dries. (See Diagram 2.) Secure the photo to the lid with photo-safe tape.

5. Place the lid on the box. Arrange memorabilia on the box and carefully secure in place with straight pins.

6. To hang the frame, find the center back of the box. Cut two $\frac{1}{8}$-inch vertical slits 3 inches apart and 2 inches from the top edge of the box. Insert brass brads in slits and splay ends. Wrap string around the brad heads several times and knot.

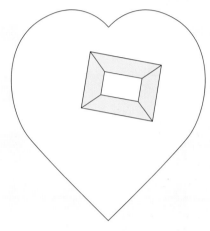

1. Create fabric flaps by cutting diagonally into the corners, working from the back of the lid.

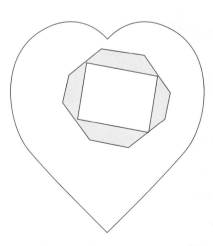

2. Wrap the fabric flaps to the back of the frame and glue in place.

Materials

Fabric-covered candy box
Pencil
Craft knife
Scissors
White glue
Straight pins
Photo-safe tape
Photo
Memorabilia such as ribbon, boutonnière, tickets, jewelry, or hair ornament
Brass brads (optional)
String (optional)

Model measures $9\frac{1}{2}$ x $9\frac{1}{2}$ x $1\frac{1}{2}$ inches.

Love in Bloom Mat

A field of delicate red roses makes the perfect mat for a romantic photo. To create a wedding keepsake for a friend, I used her favorite flower to cover a mat. The same red rosebuds also graced the walkways and tabletops at her wedding. Other types of flowers can make an equally stunning presentation. Use small flowers that retain their color, shape, and density when dried, such as yellow daisies and chrysanthemums. You can substitute small silk flowers for dried, if desired.

Materials

Frame
Black mat board
Mat-cutting equipment
Glue gun and glue sticks
Stapler (optional)
Several dozen dried rosebuds or small roses
Small gardening shears
Photo

Model measures II x II inches.

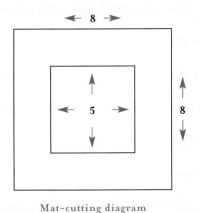

Mat-cutting diagram

1. Remove the glass, mat, and/or frame backing from the frame.

2. Cut the mat board to size (see Cutting Mats, page 15), or have a professional framer cut the mat board for you. Dimensions for the mat used in the model are shown in the diagram at left.

3. Insert the mat in the frame and secure in place with hot glue or staples. Choose roses of similar size and snip off rose stems with shears. Starting in one corner, glue the rosebuds to the mat one at a time with the glue gun. Place the rosebuds snugly together when gluing; the mat should not be visible between the flowers.

4. Insert the photo and frame backing in the frame.

Candy Corn Mat

W hen Nick (alias Peter Pan) told me that the best thing about Halloween is candy corn, I realized it offered an easy method for adding color and texture to a mat. Match other small items such as dog biscuits, game tiles, or tiny trinkets to favorite photos, then just arrange and glue in place. Other types of candy can highlight other occasions: try candy hearts for Valentine's Day, or jellybeans for Easter or springtime photos.

Materials

Frame
Cream-colored mat board
Mat-cutting equipment
Candy corn
Gold jelly beans
Varnish
Glue gun and glue sticks
Photo

Model measures 7¾ x 9½ inches.

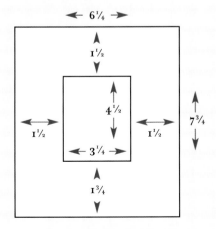

Mat-cutting diagram

1. Remove the glass, mat, and/or frame backing from the frame.

2. Cut the mat board to size (see Cutting Mats, page 15), or have a professional framer cut the mat board for you. Dimensions for the mat used in the model are shown in the diagram at left.

3. Coat the candy with varnish and let dry. (This will make it more durable and help keep it from attracting bugs.)

4. Arrange the candy corn and jelly beans on the mat. Glue in place with the glue gun.

5. Insert the mat, photo, and frame backing in the frame.

Carved Christmas Frame

The best thing about shopping at scrapbook stores is exploring the dazzling array of beautiful papers. Since I have clouds painted on the walls of my entryway, I am partial to this particular pattern, but you can adapt your own favorites to various photos. My niece floats as the focus of this cloud frame made with enchanting decorative paper, white glitter, and cotton batting.

Materials

Frame

Cloud-patterned paper, large enough to cover frame

Pencil

Ruler

Scissors

Spray adhesive

Craft knife

Cotton quilt batting

Straight pins or fabric marking pen

Poster board or foamboard

White craft glue

Spray glitter in coordinating color

Ivory card stock

Mat board, about 3 inches square

Pink satin fabric, about 3 x 5 inches

Gray paper curling ribbon, ½ yard

2 or 3 self-adhesive foam spacers

Photo

Model measures 10 x 10 inches.

1. Remove the glass, mat, and/or frame backing from the frame.

2. Cut strips of the patterned paper ¾-inch wide and as long as the length of the frame window opening. Spray the backs of the strips with spray adhesive. Press the strips in place around the edges of the window, wrapping the sides of the strips around to the front of the frame. (See Diagram 1.)

3. Measure the front surface and sides of the frame. Trim the patterned paper to that size. Measure the frame's window and mark same size window in the center of the patterned paper. With a craft knife and straightedge, trim the window from the center of the paper.

4. Spray the back of the paper with spray adhesive. Align the window opening of the paper with the frame window and carefully press the paper in place, smoothing it around the sides of the frame. Fold the corners as if wrapping a package and glue in place, or trim off the excess paper. Be sure the edges are completely adhered.

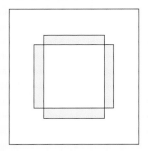

1. Wrap the edges of the frame window with strips of paper, folding the sides toward the front of the frame.

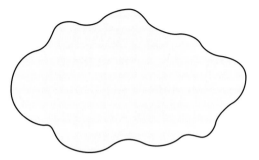

Cloud Pattern (shown actual size)

5. Measure the frame's outside dimension. Enlarge the border pattern on a photocopier so the inner edge of the cloud border fits the outer dimension of the frame. (See **A Note on the Patterns**, page 17.) To cut out the batting, either secure the pattern to the batting with pins, or trace its outline with a marking pen. Be sure to make the window opening of the batting slightly smaller than the outside dimension of the frame to achieve a snug fit.

6. Trace the border pattern onto the poster board or foamboard and cut it out with the craft knife. The window of this border piece should match the outside dimension of the frame.

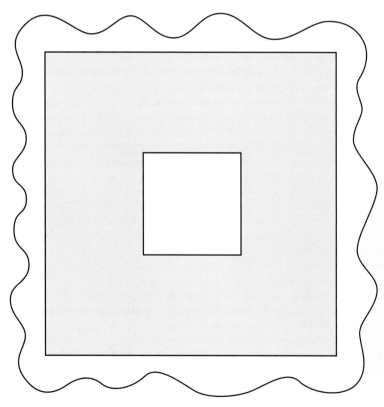

Border Pattern
(enlarge 250%)

7. Spray the back of the batting border with spray adhesive. Align it with the poster board or foamboard border and press to adhere. Place the border around the frame, keeping the batting flush with the front of the frame. Secure the border to the frame with a thin line of white craft glue on the back of the frame. Let dry.

8. Spray the frame and border with spray glitter. Let dry.

9. Print the subject's name on ivory card stock. Trace or photocopy the cloud pattern and cut it out. Center the cloud pattern over the printed name and cut out. (If you are hand lettering the name rather than printing it on the computer, trace the cloud outline onto the card stock first.) Glue the cloud to the frame with a thin layer of white craft glue.

10. Trace or photocopy the balloon pattern. Transfer to the mat board square and cut out. Cut a piece of pink satin slightly larger than this mat balloon. Notch the edges so they will fold smoothly over the curved shape. With the satin face down and the balloon mat on top (see **Diagram 2**), wrap the notched edges to the balloon back and glue them down with white craft glue. Cut an oval of satin slightly smaller than the balloon dimension and glue it to the balloon back, covering the raw edges of the turned-back notches. (See **Diagram 3**.) Let dry.

11. Tie the ribbon to the balloon and curl it. Trim the ribbon to the desired length. Stick adhesive spacers to the back of the balloon and attach it to the frame front.

12. Insert the photo and frame backing in the frame.

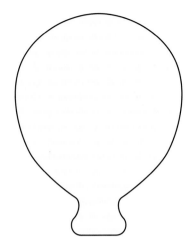

Balloon Pattern
(shown actual size)

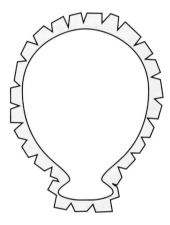

2. Place the notched satin wrong side up, then put the balloon face down on top of it.

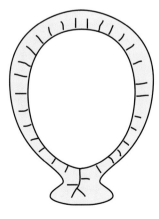

3. Fold over and glue the notched edges to the balloon, then cover them with an oval of satin.

Displaying Family Treasures

Each leaf, each flower, and each family has its own personality. Define your family's character by framing bits and pieces of family lore and enhancing photos of family life. These personal artifacts can transform the ordinariness of a house into the uniqueness of a home. Make yours a family to remember, and show off the things that make you one of a kind.

Easy Decoupage Frame

S tickers are a quick and easy way to decorate any surface. Thanks to the scrapbooking craze, they're available in virtually unlimited designs to coordinate with any theme. My ten-year-old daughter made a special gift for her teacher to commemorate her wedding day. She chose the frame, the card, and the beautiful stickers, and almost completed the project by herself. (She needed help sanding, since the printed color on stickers can be easily removed.) Try this treatment with a birthday card or a baby announcement. Or add a glossy finish and pop in a chic greeting card. Other embellishments that can be glued to a plain frame are graphics cut from magazines, or scraps of lace.

Materials

Wood frame with molded surface
Paintbrush
Black acrylic paint
Floral stickers
Sandpaper
Spray or liquid gloss sealer
Greeting card or photo

Model measures 9 x 11 inches.

1. Remove the glass, mat, and/or frame backing from the frame.

2. Apply two coats of black paint, drying thoroughly between each coat.

3. Press stickers to frame in random pattern. Make sure that all edges of the stickers adhere to the frame surface. With sandpaper, lightly sand some of the painted areas of the frame to reveal the wood. Also lightly sand some of the stickers to "age" them.

4. Apply two coats of sealer, drying thoroughly between each coat.

5. Insert the image and frame backing into the frame.

Home Sweet Home Mat

My mother displays antique leather suitcases on a special shelf in her study. I was always curious about where these suitcases had been and how many miles they had traveled. These miniature versions are the perfect way to show off the things you've done and the wonders you've seen on your travels. Add destination stickers found at scrapbook stores or shop for stickers while on vacation. (Note: Instructions are given for the frame shown center front in the photo. To make coordinating frames, follow directions and change paint colors and suede colors.)

Materials

Wood frame with dark brown finish

Tan mat board

Mat-cutting equipment

Brown acrylic paint

Paintbrush

One wooden drawer pull, 3⅝-inch wide

White craft glue

2 antique-finish brass vest buckles, 1-inch wide

2 strips of rust colored suede, each ¾ x 10 inches

Masking tape

Photo

Stickers

Center front frame measures 9 x 7 inches, excluding handle.

1. Remove the glass, mat, and/or frame backing from the frame.

2. Apply a thin coat of paint to the frame, mat, and drawer pull. To achieve a weathered look, let the wood finish of the frame show through the paint. Let dry.

3. Center the drawer pull on the top edge of the frame and glue in place. Slide the buckles onto the suede strips. Wrap the ends of the strips to the back of the frame and glue in place. Tape the ends down just until the glue dries, then carefully remove the tape.

4. Insert the mat, photo, and frame backing in the frame.

5. Place stickers on the frame and/or mat.

Once Upon a Time Mat

Celebrating Nature

The opportunity to experience the natural world is to be celebrated and recorded. When packing for vacations or even for day trips, we all bring along a camera. Professional and amateur photographers agree that nothing beats nature, and nothing beats natural light. Transport yourself to sandy shores, snowy hills, shady groves, and sunny vales with the help of these frames inspired by the great outdoors.

Sand and Shell Frame

When I go on vacation, I prefer historic cities that offer interesting architecture and plenty of museums to explore. But all my husband needs is a beach and a clear blue sky. I must admit that recalling a stroll in the sand can bring serenity to a hectic day. Change the landscape of your desk with this quick transformation of a plain frame to help you relive a relaxing moment in the sun and sand. Or create a darker textured background on the frame and adorn it with small twigs, pinecones, berries, and other treasures from a nature walk.

Materials

Frame
Beige mat board
Sand-colored textured paint (spray or brush-on)
Paintbrush (optional)
Small shells, assorted sizes and shapes
White craft glue
Photo

Model measures 9½ x 7½ inches

1. Remove the glass, mat, and/or frame backing from the frame.

2. Apply the textured paint to the frame and let dry.

3. Glue shells as desired to the frame and let dry.

4. Insert the mat, photo, and frame backing in the frame.

Water Mat

You can almost hear this miniature mermaid, and every other kid in the pool, shouting, "Watch me, Mom!" Discovering this photo pinned to a friend's bulletin board inspired me to create a splashy water mat. A small square mat is the perfect place to add embossed tiles. Explore your local home improvement store for great designer tiles to complement your photos.

Materials

Frame
Blue mat board
Pencil
Four embossed 2-inch-square tiles
Light blue acrylic paint
Paintbrush
Glue gun and glue sticks, or stapler
**Construction adhesive such as
   Liquid Nails**
Photo

Model measures 9¼ x 9¼ inches

1. Remove the glass, mat, and/or frame backing from the frame.

2. Cut the mat board to size (see **Cutting Mats,** page 15), or have a professional framer cut the mat board for you. Dimensions for the mat used in the model are shown in the diagram at right.

3. Lightly pencil a line ½ inch outside the mat window on all four sides. Paint a wavy line along this marked line. Let dry. Carefully erase the pencil lines.

4. Insert the mat in the frame and secure with hot glue or staples. Apply construction adhesive to the tile backs and position the tiles in the corners. Let dry.

5. Insert the photo and frame backing in the frame.

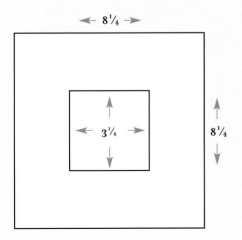

Mat-cutting diagram

Snowflake Mat

W hat is more fun in the wintertime than being safely bundled up and surrounded by snow? This photo was taken after the first big snowfall of the season when I spied my two small neighbors enjoying the excitement and wonder of a world transformed. One lacy snowflake pattern is repeated all around this wintry scene. For spring photos, use a flower silhouette. For summer, try a starfish or a nautilus shell, and for fall, make a leaf shape. Whichever shape you choose, design an image that has sections cut from the interior.

1. Remove the glass, mat, and/or frame backing from the frame.

2. Cut the mat board to size (see **Cutting Mats,** page 15), or have a professional framer cut the mat board for you. Dimensions for the mat used in the model are shown in the diagram at right.

3. Trace the snowflake pattern onto paper and carefully cut out with the craft knife.

4. Place the snowflake on the mat. Apply ink to the sponge and lightly dab it over the snowflake. (See **photos 1 and 2.**) Move the snowflake around the mat in a random pattern and repeat. Let dry.

5. Insert the mat, photo, and frame backing in the frame.

Materials

Frame
Ivory mat board
Tracing paper
Pencil
Craft knife
Blue waterproof dye-based inkpad
Cosmetic sponge
Photo

Model measures 10½ x 10 inches.

1. Gently dab the blue ink over the snowflake pattern.

2. Lift the pattern carefully, reposition it, and stencil again.

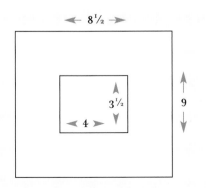

Mat-cutting diagram

← 8½ →

3½

4

9

Snowflake Pattern (enlarge 110%)

Bark and Moss Frame

W hen my brother John moved two thousand miles away, I shuffled through my old photos and chose this twenty-year-old portrait of him to display on my bookshelf. I like the trees, the natural light, and especially the eighties haircut. The warm and woodsy look of the bark and moss on the mat enhance the photo's natural setting.

Materials

Frame
Tan or brown mat board
White craft glue
Thin pieces of decorative bark
Dried moss
Photo

Model measures 6 ½ x 7 inches.

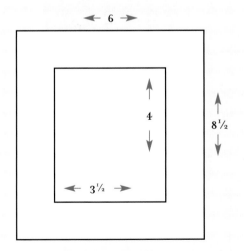

Mat-cutting diagram

1. Remove the glass, mat, and/or frame backing from the frame.

2. Cut the mat board to size (see Cutting Mats, page 15), or have a professional framer cut the mat board for you. Dimensions for the mat used in the model are shown in the diagram at right.

3. Glue the bark to the mat board, overlapping to cover the entire surface of the mat. Let dry.

4. Glue small clumps of moss over the bark. Let dry.

5. Insert the mat, photo, and frame backing in the frame.

Stamped Leaf Mat

Rose Leaves stamp uesd by permission of Rubber Stampede Inc.— A Delta Company, 2550 Pellissier Place, Whittier, CA 90601

Photo courtesy Doug Menuez/Picture Quest

orking in a garden is the ultimate high-touch activity to counter our high-tech world. Our family garden keeps growing, in more ways than one, since every year we add a new vegetable. (This year it is pumpkins.) Take a lot of photos in your garden since a leafy canopy makes a great backdrop. An easy-to-make mat brings the color and feel of the garden indoors—and it will stay green forever.

Materials

Frame
Green mat board
Leaf stamp
Green waterproof dye-based inkpad
12 wired silk leaves, each 1½ x 2¼ inches
Glue gun and glue sticks
Photo

Model measures 11½ x 1½ inches.

1. Remove the glass, mat, and/or frame backing from the frame.

2. Cut the mat board to size (see **Cutting Mats**, page 15), or have a professional framer cut the mat board for you. Dimensions for the mat used in the model are shown in the diagram at right.

3. Stamp the leaf in a random pattern over the entire surface of the mat. Let dry.

4. Bend each leaf ½ inch from the bottom end. Arrange the leaves around the edge of the mat window, wrapping the short ends to the back. Glue in place.

5. Insert the mat, photo, and frame backing in the frame.

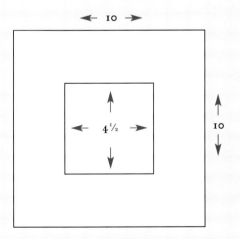

Mat-cutting diagram

Sun Catcher Frame

If you're like me, you spend a large part of your life standing in front of the kitchen sink. To brighten up this workspace, I fashioned a cheery ornament to hang in the window. This sunny smile is captured between two panes of glass and two wood frames. Keep in mind that since the finished frame is hung from ribbon, weight may be a factor, so it's best to choose frames 6 x 8 inches or smaller. Select a photo with an easily silhouetted figure, and copy it on a color photocopier. (Copy paper will allow some sunlight to show through, but photo paper is too opaque.)

Materials

Two identical frames with glass
Lavender acrylic paint
Paintbrush
Scrap paper
Painter's tape
Silver spray paint
Photo
Craft knife
Pencil
Tracing paper
Transfer paper
Stencil paper
Spray adhesive
Green spray paint
Green vellum paper
4 white chenille stems
White craft glue
Lavender organza ribbon, ³⁄₁₆-inch
 wide, 1 yard
2 square white beads, about ¹⁄₄ wide
Sturdy cup hook

Model measures 7³⁄₄ x 5³⁄₄ inches.

1. Remove the glass, mats, and/or frame backings from the frames.

2. With lavender acrylic paint, paint both frames entirely—front, back, sides, inside edge of window, and rabbet. (See Anatomy of a Frame, page 12.) Let dry.

3. With scrap paper and tape, mask off the fronts of the frames, leaving ³⁄₈ inch exposed around the edges. Press edge of tape down firmly so paint does not seep underneath. With silver spray paint, spray the exposed borders on frame fronts, and spray the sides of the frames. Let dry. Carefully remove the tape.

4. With a craft knife, trim the photo so the subject is silhouetted.

Leaf Patterns
(shown actual size)

5. Trace the stencil pattern on tracing paper, and transfer it to the stencil paper with transfer paper. Using a craft knife, cut out the stencil and spray the back with spray adhesive.

6. With the trimmed photo right side up on the work surface, center one pane of glass over the image. Place the stencil on the glass, adhesive side down. (Do not let the stencil overlap the area of the photo image.) Mask off any exposed areas of glass. Lightly spray over the leaf stencil with green spray paint. Move the stencil and repeat to create a random pattern. Let dry.

7. Remove the photo from beneath the glass and spray the back of the photo with spray adhesive. Press in place on top of the painted glass.

8. Transfer the leaf patterns to the green vellum and cut 5 leaves. Arrange on the glass in a random pattern, overlapping the stenciled leaves if desired.

9. Cut the chenille stem to fit the long sides of the rabbet. Glue in place with white glue. (See **Diagram 1**.) Let dry. (The chenille stems act as spacers to ensure close contact between the glass panes.)

10. Place one frame on the work surface, wrong side up. Place the glass with the photo and leaves in the frame. Fold the ribbon in half lengthwise. Tie an overhand knot near the fold, creating 2-inch loop. Tape it to the frame. (See **Diagram 2**.)

11. Place the second, clear pane glass on top of the first. Apply a generous amount of white glue to the wrong side of the first frame, but keep it away from the edges so it doesn't seep out. Place the second frame on top of the first, right side up. Align the edges of the frames and press together to create tight contact. Let dry.

12. Slide the beads onto the ends of the ribbon. Trim the ribbon ends to desired length. Hang in a window from a sturdy cup hook.

1. Glue a piece of chenille stem into each rabbet of the frames. (Dotted lines represent chenille stems.)

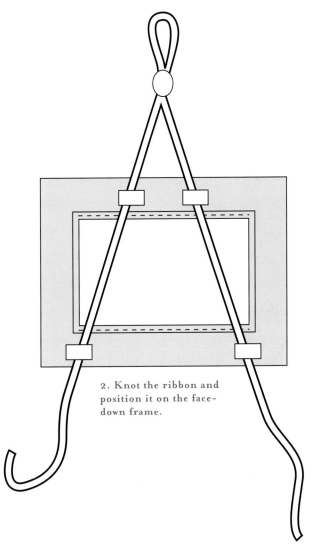

2. Knot the ribbon and position it on the face-down frame.

"To look backward for a while is to refresh the eye,
to restore it, and to render it more fit for its
prime function of looking forward."

—Margaret Fairless Barber

Honoring
Your Heritage

Who doesn't appreciate the power of a purposeful young gaze, or the tenderness in an aged, sun-baked face? Tone-on-tone antique photos are truly treasures from the past—too meaningful to hide in a drawer. Display them proudly in frames that enhance their significance. Chose heritage photos that are free from background clutter. Also, when possible, chose three-dimensional design elements that relate to the integrity of the person and of the times.

Tennis Racket Frame

A well-aged racket makes a charming frame to accent shelves in the family room or den. Aluminum tennis rackets just don't have the touch or the appeal of the old wooden rackets, which look even better with chipped paint and worn leather handles. Other sports gear might also serve as clever frames to display photos celebrating friendly competition: try Ping-Pong paddles, snowshoes, and even fishing creels. Make sure the item has a few nicks and scrapes to give it some character.

Materials

Mat-cutting equipment
Photo
Mat board
Spray adhesive
Hole punch
Wooden tennis racket
Rayon cord, 12 inches

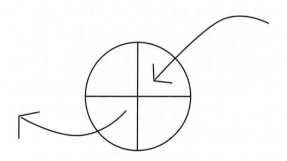

Thread the cord diagonally through an intersection in the racket strings.

1. Trim the photo to the desired size.

2. Cut the mat board slightly larger than the photo ($\frac{1}{4}$ to $\frac{1}{2}$ inch larger on all sides). Spray the back of the photo with spray adhesive. Center the photo on the mat board and press in place to adhere.

3. Punch one hole in the top left corner and one in the bottom right corner of the mat board.

4. Place the mat on the racket face. Line up the punched holes over intersections of racket strings.

5. Cut the rayon cord in half. Thread one piece of cord through a hole from the top, then run it beneath the string intersection, and back up through hole. (See diagram.) Tie a knot in the cord. Repeat with second piece of cord.

Bead-Embellished Mat

This lovely portrait of my late mother-in-law was originally bordered by a plain ivory mat, which has now been given a facelift with sparkling glass beads. This technique only looks complex—it's really quite easy. Double-sided adhesive replaces needle and thread for a treatment that flatters any smile.

1. Remove the glass, mat, and/or frame backing from the frame.

2. Cut the mat board to size (see **Cutting Mats**, page 15), or have a professional framer cut the mat board for you. Dimensions for the mat used in the model are shown in the diagram at right.

3. From adhesive sheets cut 1½-inch strips. Piece the strips to create a border around the mat window and trim to fit. Peel the backing from the strips and stick in place. Using the pattern on page 111 as a guide, mark the embellishment design on the protective layer of adhesive with the marking pen. With a craft knife, cut lightly along the marked lines, cutting only the protective layer of adhesive. IMPORTANT: Do not cut into the mat board.

4. With the tip of the craft knife, gently pry up the protective layer from the wavy inside borders. Sprinkle purple beads evenly over the exposed adhesive. Lift mat from work surface and carefully brush

excess beads onto paper or shoebox lid. Return excess beads to container.

5. Repeat step 4, this time revealing the adhesive on the outside borders and sprinkling the silver micro beads. Repeat again for the corners, using the mixed beads.

6. Insert the mat, photo, and frame backing in the frame.

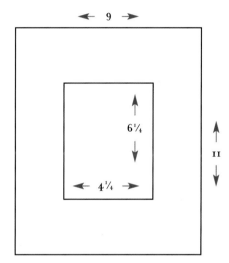

Mat-cutting diagram

Materials

Frame
Cream-colored mat board
Mat-cutting equipment
Double-sided adhesive sheet, 11 x 18 inches
Fine-tip marking pen
Purple glass mini beads
Silver micro beads
Mixed beads: silver, white, and pearl mini and bugle beads
Scrap paper or shoebox lid for catching excess beads

Model measures 10 x 12 inches.

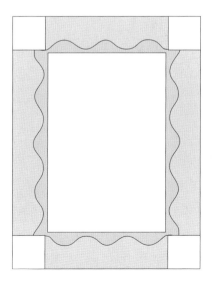

Bead Design Layout
(see page 111 for full-size pattern)

When I visit second-hand stores or flea markets, I head straight for the jewelry section. It's amusing to see how women choose to adorn themselves, and what ends up being discarded. Often you'll find pins with no pin backs and earrings with broken clasps. These flashy, well-used pieces are perfect to include in small jewelry mosaics that will make your favorite portrait sparkle. Just be sure the jewelry you choose does not have any antique value.

Materials

Small frame with broad surface area
Costume jewelry: pins and earrings
Small pliers
Mosaic adhesive
Brush
Synthetic pearls
Paper or masking tape
Spray adhesive
Mixed beads: silver mini, micro,
    and bugle beads

Model measures 5 x 4¼ inches.

1. Remove the glass, mat, and/or frame backing from the frame.

2. Using small pliers, remove any pin backs and/or earring clips from the jewelry. Arrange the jewelry on the work surface into a rough layout for the frame.

3. Brush mosaic adhesive on the frame front about $^1/_{16}$ to $^1/_8$ inch thick. (More adhesive may be needed for convex jewelry backs.) Place jewelry on frame front to cover the entire surface, filling in with loose pearls as needed. Let dry.

4. Cover large jewelry pieces with paper shapes or masking tape. Spray the frame front with spray adhesive. Sprinkle mixed beads over exposed areas. Carefully brush off excess beads. Remove paper or tape.

5. Insert the photo and frame backing in the frame.

Blended Clay Frame

Twist and fold ordinary polymer clay to simulate gleaming semiprecious stone. This iridescent clay veneer became an ideal complement to a much-loved photo of my maternal grandmother as a young child. The distinct dark hues of the clay enhance the black-and-white tones of the photo. (Note: The frame will be placed in an oven to bake the clay, so it must be heat-safe and contain no plastic parts. See page 11 for more on working with polymer clay.)

Materials

Heat-safe frame with raised decorative border around window
Polymer clay, 2-ounce packages:
   3 tan, 1 purple, 1 black
Waxed paper
Acrylic clay roller or rolling pin
Polymer clay blade
Metal ruler or straightedge
Large glass pan or metal baking sheet
Old metal spoon (optional)
Liquid sealer
Paintbrush
Patterned paper
Craft knife
Necklace
Photo-safe tape
4 self-adhesive foam spacers

Model measures 8 x 10 inches.

1. Remove the glass, mat, and/or frame backing from the frame.

2. Condition the tan clay by kneading until soft, then place it on the work surface. Place a piece of waxed paper over the clay and roll it flat. Repeat for the remaining colors, using only half a package of the black. Roll the clay to various thicknesses from $1/8$ to $1/2$ inch. Cut the sheets into strips 3 or 4 inches wide. Layer the strips in random order, then twist and fold the layers together. (See **Photo 1**.) Do not blend the colors completely; striations should be visible.

1. Twist and fold the clay layers together until a swirling pattern emerges.

2. Slice the blended clay into ¼-inch disks.

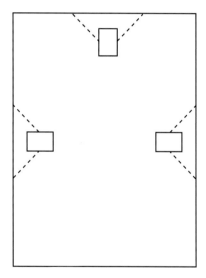

With photo-safe tape, secure the necklace to the back of the photo.

3. With the blade, slice through clay to make cross sections of blended clay approximately ¼ inch thick. (See **Photo 2**.) Place the sections side by side on the work surface, cover with a piece of waxed paper, and roll together to make one large sheet of clay approximately ⅛ to 3/16 inch thick. Remove the waxed paper.

4. With a metal ruler as a guide, cut strips of clay wide enough to cover the frame. Press the strips over the frame, butting them up to the raised border and wrapping the clay around the outside edges of the frame. Where the strips meet, press them together and smooth with fingers. When the surface is completely covered, use the blade to trim away the excess clay.

5. Place the clay-covered frame in a pan or on a baking sheet and bake according to the clay manufacturer's directions. Monitor the clay while in the oven and if any bubbles appear during baking, carefully flatten them with the back of a spoon. Let cool.

6. Brush on a coat of sealer. Let dry. Repeat with second coat.

7. Cut patterned paper to fit in window of frame. Insert patterned paper and frame backing in the frame. Tape the necklace chain to the back of the photo (see **diagram**). Stick foam spacers to photo back at corners. Attach the photo to the center of the frame.

The penny quilt motif is a time-tested favorite, and here the little circles serve as mini-frames for found objects. Seated behind the reins of his sled, the man in this image appears at home, much more so than if he had been posing stiffly against a cloth backdrop. Perhaps his shirt pocket contained tokens like the ones stitched to this fuzzy felt mat: pennies, washers, bits of leather. Choose items for your mat based on history and sentiment, or simply on shape, texture, and color.

Materials

Frame

Brown mat board

Mat-cutting equipment

Tracing paper

Pencil

Scissors

Straight pins

Felt, 9 x 12-inch pieces: 1 taupe, 1 tan, 1 brown

Embroidery floss: medium brown, light gray

Needle

Decorative accents such as pennies, metal washers, leather scraps, buttons, or metal nuts

Double-sided tape

8–12 self-adhesive foam spacers

Model measures 12½ x 10½ inches.

1. Remove the glass, mat, and/or frame backing from the frame.

2. Cut the mat board to size (see Cutting Mats, page 15), or have a professional framer cut the mat board for you. Dimensions for the mat used in the model are shown in the diagram below. IMPORTANT: Do not cut a window in the mat.

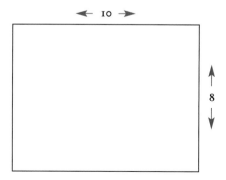

Mat-cutting diagram

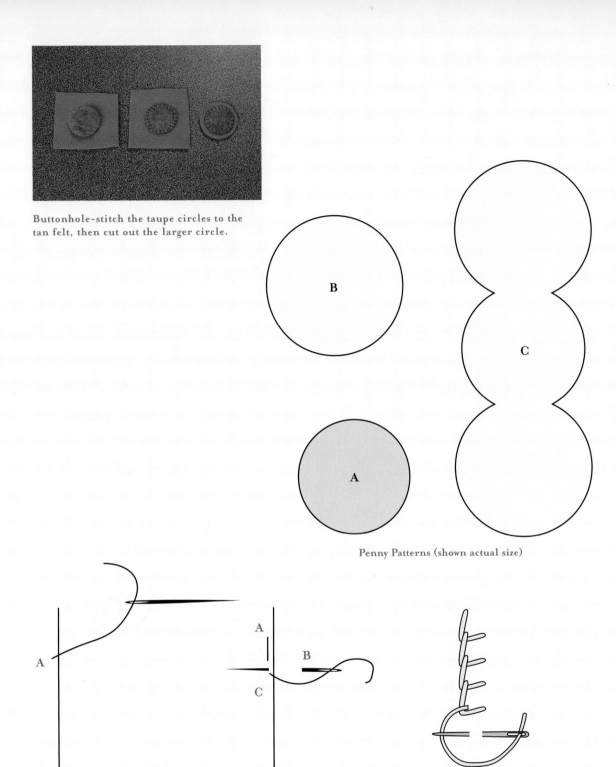

Buttonhole-stitch the taupe circles to the
tan felt, then cut out the larger circle.

B

C

A

Penny Patterns (shown actual size)

A

A
B
C

1. To make a buttonhole stitch, bring the needle up at A, down at B, and back up at C. Bring the thread
under the needle at C, pull the needle through until the thread lies flat but is not too tight. Continue in
this manner until the stitches go all the way around the felt circle.

3. Trace patterns A, B, and C.

4. Using pattern A, cut 8 circles from taupe felt and pin them to the piece of tan felt. With two strands of brown floss, attach the circles to the tan felt with buttonhole stitches. (See **Diagram 1**.) Center pattern B, the large circle, over the small stitched circles and cut out. (See **photo**.)

5. Using pattern A, cut 8 more circles from taupe felt. Pin pairs of circles to tan felt, leaving 1⅜ inches between them. With two strands of brown floss, attach the circles to the tan felt with buttonhole stitches, as before. Center pattern C over the stitched pairs (with a blank circle in the middle of the pattern) and cut out.

6. Pin the stitched pieces in place on the piece of brown felt, following the layout

as a guide. (See **Diagram 2**.) With two strands of gray embroidery floss, attach the stitched pieces to the brown felt with buttonhole stitches.

7. With brown embroidery floss, stitch the decorative accents to the centers of the circles. (See **Diagram 3**.)

8. Cut a window in the center of the brown felt, 1 inch smaller all around than the photo. Center the design over the mat and wrap the felt around the board. Trim excess felt from corners if desired. Tape the wrapped edges of the felt to the back of the mat board. Stick adhesive spacers to the exposed mat board around the edge of the cut window, without touching the felt. Attach photo to spacers.

9. Insert the mat, photo, and frame backing in the frame.

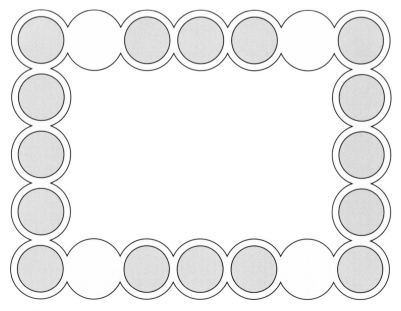

3. To attach found objects without holes, stitch diagonally across the item about three times.

2. Use this layout diagram as a guide when placing the stitched pieces on the brown background piece.

Crazy Quilt Mat

S ome histories are recorded with words and some are recorded with millions of tiny stitches. Did the fabric square once belong to a larger quilt that adorned a velvet chair or warmed tired shoulders? As with most antique crazy quilts, there is history recorded in the stitches of this mat. The purple velvet scraps were snipped from a tablecloth that belonged to my paternal grandparents. I wanted a dark palette with similar values, so I chose dark fabrics with a variety of textures. The two lapel pins attached as accents are reproductions, but they resemble the jewelry that my grandmother always sported. Since this work was inspired by the Victorian craze for crazy quilts, I decided to display it using the popular quilting approach of turning a square into a diamond by rotating it forty-five degrees, referred to as "on point."

Materials

Frame

Black mat board

Mat-cutting equipment

Scraps of velvet and cotton: black, brown, burgundy, magenta, purple, sage green

Straight pins

Sewing thread in contrasting colors

Sewing machine or hand-sewing needle

Fabric marker

7-inch square of white cotton fabric

Iron and ironing board

Double-sided tape

Glue gun and glue sticks

Antique or reproduction hat or lapel pins

Model measures 10 x 10 inches.

1. Remove the glass, mat, and/or frame backing from the frame.

2. Cut the mat board to size (see Cutting Mats, page 15), or have a professional framer cut the mat board for you. Dimensions for the mat used in the model are shown in the diagram below.

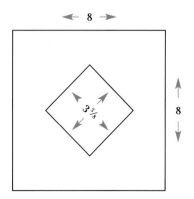

Mat-cutting diagram

Top

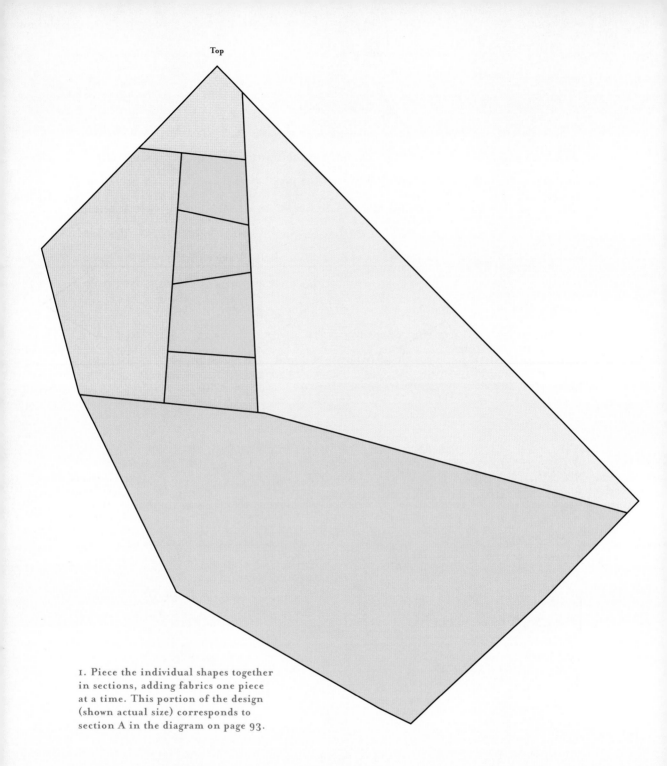

1. Piece the individual shapes together
in sections, adding fabrics one piece
at a time. This portion of the design
(shown actual size) corresponds to
section A in the diagram on page 93.

Right Corner

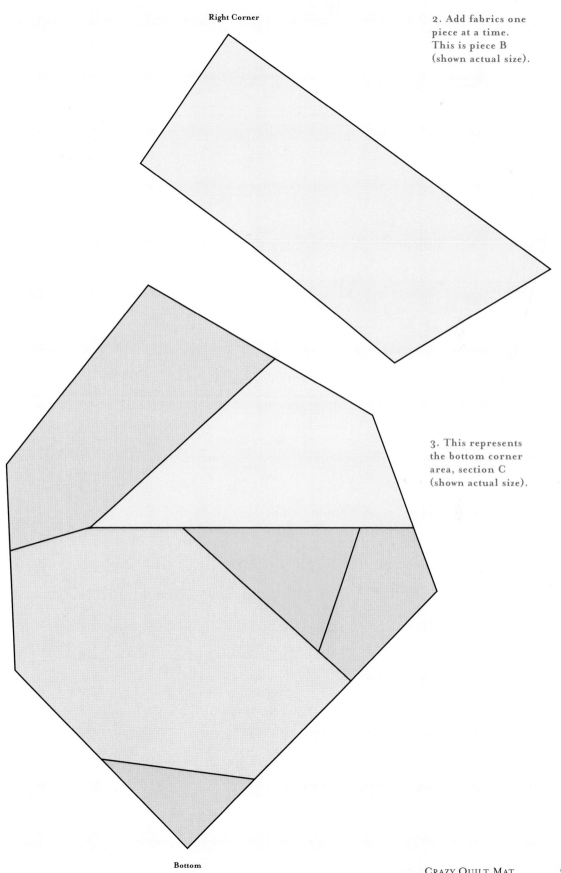

2. Add fabrics one piece at a time. This is piece B (shown actual size).

3. This represents the bottom corner area, section C (shown actual size).

Bottom

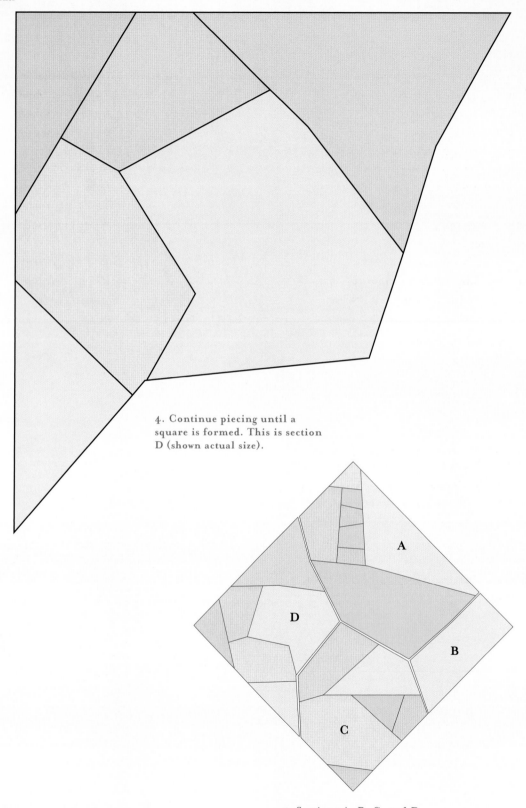

4. Continue piecing until a
square is formed. This is section
D (shown actual size).

5. Sections A, B, C, and D
pieced together (shown at
30 percent of actual size).

3. To create your own original crazy quilt square, cut scraps of fabric into small, irregular pieces. (Remember to add ¼ inch on all sides of each individual piece for seam allowance.) Arrange the pieces in a random pattern with the edges overlapping, to make square measuring at least 8½ x 8½ inches. (Follow **Diagrams I through 4** to re-create the look of the square shown here.) With right sides together, machine- or hand-stitch the fabrics together. Begin with the largest piece, building the quilt in four sections, then stitch the sections together to form a square. (See **Diagram 5**.) Press the seams flat as you work.

4. Using the fabric marker, in the center of the wrong side of the pieced square, draw a 3⅜-inch square on the diagonal. (See **Diagram 6**.) Center the white fabric on the right side of the pieced square and pin them together. Stitch along the marked line. (Refer to the photos illustrating Step 3 in the **Burlap Mat project**, pages 51-53.) Trim out the center of the stitched square. Cut diagonals into the corners, but be careful not to cut the stitching. Turn the fabric right side out and press.

5. Insert the mat between the pieced square and the white fabric. Place the assembly wrong side up and tape the white fabric to the back of the mat, pulling the fabric taut so the pieced fabric wraps slightly around the window to the back and no white fabric shows on the front.

6. Apply a thin line of glue along the outer edges of the right side of the mat and pull the pieced fabric taut over the board to create flat surface. Hold the fabric edges in place in place briefly until the hot glue dries. Trim the pieced square even with the outside edges of the mat.

7. Insert the mat and photo in the frame. Pin the hat or lapel pins in place.

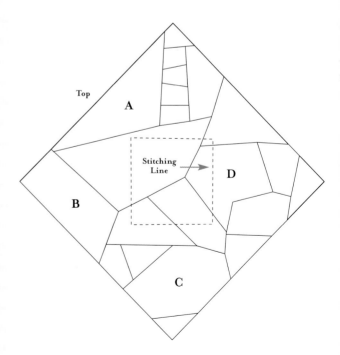

6. On the back of the fabric, mark a 3⅜-inch square that is positioned diagonally in relation to the fabric square.

"Whatever beauty may be, it has for its basis order, and for its essence, unity."

—Father Andre

Enhancing Your Collections

Silver jewelry, postage stamps, architectural fragments, antique buttons, bits of ribbon, dried leaves, even old subway tokens—do we collect because of aesthetics or emotion? Perhaps for both reasons. If the things that you love are fairly small and relatively flat, it's time to take them off of the shelves and out of the boxes and pop them into frames for everyone to enjoy. A variety of techniques allow you to turn the walls of your home into a museum of serendipity.

Distressed Frames

M y family discovered this treatment by accident when my daughters were painting watercolor landscapes. When they ran out of paper, they painted the other items on the table, including these three frames. Watercolor paint works wonderfully as a stain on porous surfaces, and it has an attractive mat finish when dried. Just splatter on a contrasting color and sand the corners and exposed edges. Then dust off your old maps and antique prints to display in these newly aged frames. Instructions are given for the small green frame; to make coordinating frames, just change the paint colors. (Note: You will need a pine frame, because it is porous enough to accept watercolor. Harder woods will resist the paint and the hues will be weak.)

Materials

Pine frame

Watercolor paint: dark green, light green, dark blue

Paintbrush

Toothbrush or short-bristled paintbrush

Sandpaper

Artwork

Small frame measures 7½ x 6 inches.

1. Remove the glass, mat, and/or frame backing from the frame.

2. Using a high concentration of water color for strong hues, paint the frame with one coat of dark green paint. Let dry. Paint the frame with one coat of light green paint. Let dry.

3. Using a toothbrush or short-bristled paintbrush, splatter dark blue paint over the frame. To splatter, load the brush with paint and run your thumb across the end of the bristles. (Be sure the work surface is well protected from excess splatters.) Let dry.

4. Sand the corners and around the window edges of the frame to reveal some wood.

5. Insert the artwork and frame backing in the frame.

Spun Gold Mats

Single images such as these antique fruit prints look great surrounded by wide square mats. These mats were enhanced with a fast, fun, and foolproof dipping technique that yields instant results and tempts you to use it on everything in sight. The first time I tried this, I dipped mats, a glass vase, straw placemats, even plastic hair clips. Try it! You'll feel like a modern-day King Midas.

1. Remove the glass, mat, and/or frame backing from the frame.

2. Cut the mat board to size (see **Cutting Mats, page 15**), or have a professional framer cut the mat board for you. Dimensions for the mat used in the model are shown in the diagram at right.

3. Place the plastic liner in the pan. Fill the pan with water. Spray some gold paint on the surface of the water. (See **Photo 1**.) Quickly dip the mat, face down, onto the paint. (See **Photo 2**.) Carefully lift the mat from the water. (See **Photo 3**.) Place the mat on newspaper to dry. If the mat begins to warp, place it between paper towels and weigh it down with a stack of books; leave overnight.

4. To hang as shown, tie ribbons in single knots around top edge of frame, one at each corner. Wrap ribbon ends around the twig and stitch in place. Trim ends.

5. Insert the mat, artwork, and frame backing in the frame.

Materials

Frame

Black mat board

Plastic liner (13-gallon plastic garbage bag works well)

Shallow pan, at least 10 inches wide

Gold spray paint

Newspaper

Artwork

Gold velvet ribbon, ¾-inch wide, two 9-inch lengths (optional)

Large twig (optional)

Needle and matching thread (optional)

Model measures 11 x 11 inches.

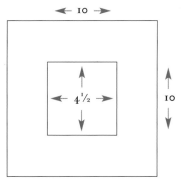

Mat-cutting diagram

1. Gently spray gold paint onto the water's surface.

2. Quickly dip the mat, face down, onto the paint.

3. Carefully lift the mat from the water.

Tin Tile Frame

After renovating an old house, I was left with a box of goodies: bits of egg-and-dart molding, turned finials, and extra tin ceiling tiles. A shiny tin tile can easily be transformed into a snappy frame. Add a faux-vintage work of art, or if you're lucky, add some genuine vintage art. These tiles can be purchased individually at craft and home-improvement stores. (Note: Since the tiles are 12-inch squares, the total measurement of the frame, including the side edges, must be less than 12 inches.)

1. Remove the glass, mat, and/or frame backing from the frame.

2. Measure the surface and side of the frame. Add the surface measurement to two side measurements, plus ⅛-inch allowance for bending. With pencil and metal ruler, draw a square of this total measurement centered on the tin tile. With tin snips, trim excess tin. Cut square notches at the corners. (See diagram.)

3. Measure the width of the frame window, then *subtract* the total measurements of the side depth as well as ⅛-inch allowance for bending on all sides. For example, if the window is 5 inches square and the side depth is ½ inch, cut a 2½-inch square out of the tile center (5 inches minus 2 inches for total side depths minus ½ inch for total bending allowance.) Mark this measurement in the tile center and cut it out. Cut diagonal lines into the corners. (See diagram.)

4. Apply a thin layer of adhesive to frame front. Center the trimmed tile on the frame and press in place. (See diagram.) Let dry. Carefully bend down outer edges of the tin to conform to frame shape. With a hammer, nail tacks on frame sides, at corners and about 1½ inches apart along the sides.

5. Apply a thin layer of adhesive to the frame window sides. Carefully bend down the inner edges of the tin and hold in place until it adheres to the wood. If desired, hammer tacks on frame front.

6. If you want to highlight the tile's texture, paint the frame with acrylic paint. When dry, remove paint with a damp cloth, leaving small amounts on the textured areas.

7. Insert the artwork and frame backing in the frame.

Materials

One 12-inch ornamental tin ceiling tile
Pencil
Metal ruler
Tin snips
**Construction adhesive such as
    Liquid Nails**
10-inch frame with flat surface
Hammer
Silver-colored tacks
Acrylic paint (optional)
Paintbrush (optional)
Scrap cloth (optional)
Artwork

Model measures 10 x 10 inches.

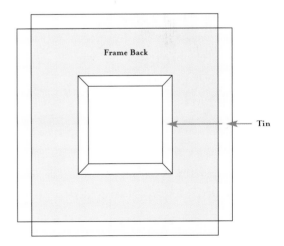

Notch the tile's outer corners, and cut diagonals into the window corners. After applying glue, center the frame face down over the trimmed tile.

Broken Dishes Frame

Childhood equals magic, even for children who have long since grown up. The doll and dishes seen here belong to a very old friend who remembers tea parties of red Kool-Aid and Ritz crackers. Mosaic frames are the perfect way to display such sentimental possessions and to keep tea parties alive forever. (Note: To break a dish safely, place it in an old pillowcase to contain the shards and hit it gently with a hammer.)

1. Remove the glass, mat, and/or frame backing from the frame.

2. Arrange the dish pieces on the frame surfaces, fitting them closely together. (See **photo.**) Glue in place with mosaic adhesive. Let dry overnight.

3. Mask off untiled areas with masking tape. Mix grout according to manufacturer's directions. (Grout should be the consistency of mashed potatoes.) Apply grout to tiled area, working it between the tiles with a sponge. Wipe off excess and let dry. Wipe off grout film with damp sponge.

4. Dilute acrylic paint with water in 1:1 proportions and apply unevenly to grout. Wipe off excess paint with damp sponge.

5. If displaying objects on fabric, cut foamboard to fit frame opening. Cover with fabric, notching edges and wrapping to back of board (refer to the diagrams illustrating Step 10 in the **Cloud Frame project,** page 32-35). Glue fabric to board back. Insert covered board and frame backing in frame. Arrange objects and glue to fabric with mosaic adhesive. Let dry.

6. If displaying objects on mat board, cut mat board to fit frame opening. Insert mat board and frame backing in frame. Arrange objects and glue to mat with mosaic adhesive. Let dry.

Materials

Wood frames with dark finish
Broken dish pieces
Mosaic adhesive
Masking tape
White grout and mixing container
Sponge
Tan acrylic paint
Paintbrush
Blue fabric or mat board
Foamboard (optional)
White craft glue
Objects for display

Model frames measure 6½ x 9 inches and 13 x 9½ inches.

Arrange the broken pieces so they fit closely together on the frame.

Bamboo Frames

To show off my modest collection of Asian artifacts, I wanted some avant-garde but easy and inexpensive frames. The bamboo sticks add an air of authenticity, and also lend an interesting silhouette to a plain square frame. This look works equally well in Asian, contemporary, and Mission-style interiors. (Note: Instructions are given for the lavender frame. To make coordinating frames, change color of topcoat paint; also change floss colors if desired.)

Materials

Wood frame
Acrylic paint: cream, lavender
Paintbrush
Sandpaper
Utility knife
**Bamboo (1 package contains 10–12
    sticks, about 36 inches long)**
White craft glue
Embroidery floss: gold, lavender
Artwork

Model measures 13 x 13 inches.

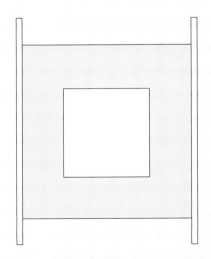

1. Glue one bamboo stick to each vertical side of the frame, centered along the frame edge.

1. Remove the glass, mat, and/or frame backing from the frame.

2. Apply one coat of cream paint to the frame. While the paint is still wet, use the blunt end of the paintbrush to create a swirling pattern in the paint. Let dry.

3. Paint over the cream paint with the lavender paint. While the paint is still wet, repeat the swirling process. Let dry.

4. Sand the surface of the frame to reveal areas of cream paint and/or wood beneath the lavender paint.

5. With a utility knife, cut eight sticks of bamboo, each approximately $3\frac{1}{3}$ inches longer than the sides of the frame. Glue one piece of bamboo to each vertical side of the frame, so that it protrudes equally from the top and bottom. Let dry. (See Diagram 1.)

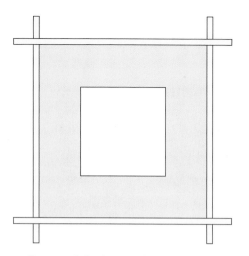

2. On top of the first sticks, secure a crosswise pair of sticks with embroidery floss.

6. Place one bamboo stick across the top and the bottom edges of the frame, on top of the first two sticks. (See **Diagram 2**.) With gold embroidery floss, wrap tightly at the intersections to secure the upper sticks to the lower sticks. Knot the floss at the back.

7. Place another stick at each side of the frame, beneath the horizontal sticks. (See **Diagram 3**.) With gold embroidery floss, wrap tightly at the intersections to secure the upper sticks to the lower sticks. Knot the floss at the back.

8. Place another stick across the top and the bottom edges of the frame, on top of the vertical sticks. (See **Diagram 4**.) With lavender embroidery floss, wrap tightly at the intersections to secure the upper sticks to the lower sticks. Knot the floss at the back.

9. Insert the artwork and frame backing in the frame.

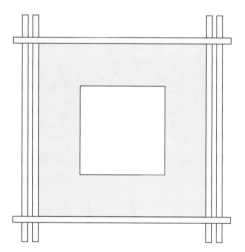

3. Secure a another pair of sticks along the vertical edges, beneath the horizontal ones.

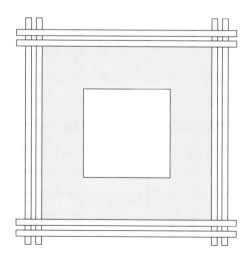

4. Attach the final pair of horizontal sticks on top of the vertical ones.

Marbled Shadowbox Frame

This sleight-of-hand crafting technique will quickly become one of your
favorites. Long used as endpaper and wallpaper, marbled paper can now
line your shadow box frame. I have impressed many jaded school children
over the years with this method of transferring floating colors from starch to
paper. Each page is a one-of-a-kind effort, worthy of showcasing historic
treasures. Try this foolproof technique to fashion a classic.

Materials

2 frames (smaller frame must fit inside
    larger frame)

Mat board

Mat-cutting equipment

Old newspapers

Shallow pan large enough to
    accommodate paper

Plastic liner (13-gallon plastic garbage
    bag works well)

Liquid starch

Acrylic paint: rust, teal, purple

3 mixing containers

3 plastic spoons to stir paint

3 glass or plastic eyedroppers

Instrument to manipulate paint, such
    as fork, comb, or feather

3 sheets pink paper, each 9 x 12 inches
    or larger

Iron and ironing board

Scrap of white cloth

Craft knife

Spray adhesive

White craft glue

Green silk ribbon, 24 inches

Memorabilia for display

Double-sided tape

Model measures 12½ x 10½ inches.

1. Remove the glass, mat, and/or frame backing from the frame.

2. Cut the mat board to size to fit the large frame (see **Cutting Mats, page 15**), or have a professional framer cut the mat board for you. Dimensions for the mat used in the model are shown in the diagram below. IMPORTANT: Do not cut a window in the mat.

3. Spread out some newspapers so they will be ready for drying the marbled paper. Place the plastic liner in the pan. Pour about ¾ to 1 inch of starch into the pan. Dilute the paints with water, approximately 1 part paint to 2 parts water. (Note: You may need to experiment with proportions of paint to water. The surface tension of the starch allows the paint to float, but if the paint is not diluted enough it will be too heavy and will sink to the bottom of the pan.)

4. Drop single drops of paint on top of the starch (See **Photo 1**.) Carefully manipulate the paint in desired pattern with a fork or other instrument. (See **Photo 2**.) Do not

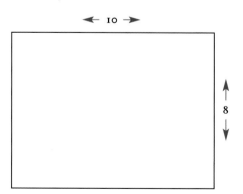

Mat-cutting diagram

dip the instrument too deeply into the starch. Carefully place a sheet of paper on top of the starch with a slight rolling motion; do not plunk it down flat. (See **Photo 3**.) Gently peel the paper off the starch. (See **Photo 4**.) Place the paper paint side up on the newspapers. Squeegee the excess starch from the marbled paper with strips of newspaper. Let dry.

5. Squeegee the leftover paint from the starch surface with strips of newspaper and repeat Step 4 with remaining paper.

6. After paper has dried thoroughly, flatten it by pressing with a hot iron on the wrong side of the paper. Use a scrap of cloth beneath the paper to prevent any transfer of color to the ironing board.

7. Trim the marbled paper to fit the mat board. Spray the back of the trimmed paper with spray adhesive and press it in place on the mat board.

1. With an eyedropper, drop single drops of each paint color over the starch.

2. Use a fork, comb, or feather to manipulate the paint into a pattern.

3. Gently roll the paper onto the surface of the starch.

4. Carefully peel the marbled paper off the surface of the starch.

8. Cut strips of the remaining paper wide enough to wrap around the front and sides of the small frame to the frame back, and long enough to extend ¾ inch off the edges of the frame. Spray the backs of the strips with spray adhesive. Place the strips on the small frame, overlapping the corners. (See **diagram**.) With a craft knife, miter the corners by cutting through both layers of paper with one cut. Carefully remove the cut-off ends of the paper and press the strips in place, wrapping the paper around the sides of the frame to the back. With white glue, glue the paper edges to the back of the frame and to the inside of the frame window. Let dry.

9. Cut four lengths of ribbon, each long enough to wrap across the corner of the frame. Apply a small amount of white glue to the ribbon ends. Wrap the ribbons across corners and glue the ends to the back of the frame. Let dry.

10. Insert the covered mat board and the frame backing in the large frame. Apply a thin layer of white glue to the back of the small frame. Insert the small frame in the large frame and let dry.

11. Arrange the memorabilia in the frame and secure it with double-sided tape.

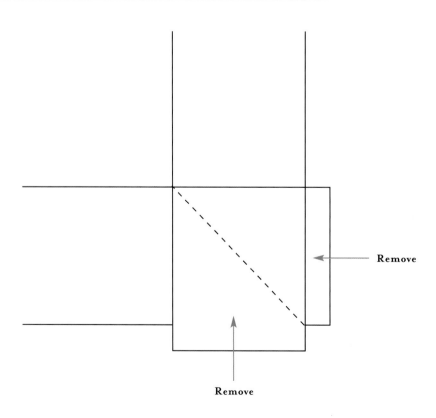

Miter the corners by cutting through both layers of paper with one cut.

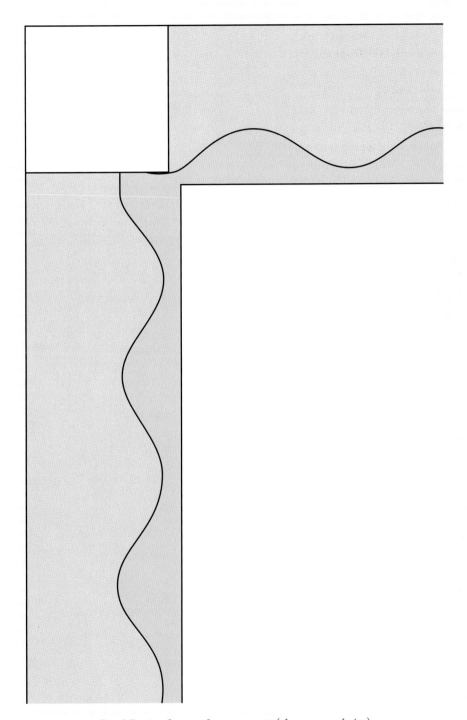

Bead Design Layout from page 75 (shown actual size)

Index

A
Adhesives, 11
Assembly, 16–17

B
Balloon pattern, 35
Bamboo Frames, 104–6
Bark and Moss Frame, 62–63
Bead-Embellished Mat, 74–75, 111
Beads, mini and micro, 11
Birthday Present Frame, 29–31
Botanicals, dried, 22–23, 51
Box frames
    birthday present, 29–31
    candy box, 20–21
    shadowbox, 107–10
Broken Dishes Frame, 102–3
Burlap Mat, 51–53
Buttonhole stitch, 86

C
Calligraphy
    Chenille Script Mat, 44–45
    Home Sweet Home Mat, 40–42
Candy box frames, 20–21
Candy Corn Mat, 24–25
Carved Christmas Frame, 26–28
Chenille Script Mat, 44–45
Chenille stems
    lettering with, 44–45
    as spacers, 69
Christmas frame, 26–28
Clay frames
    blended, 78–80
    carved, 26–28
    materials and supplies, 11
    mosaic, 81–83
Cloud Frame, 32–35
Collections, framing, 95–111
    Bamboo Frames, 104–6
    Broken Dishes Frame, 102–3
    Distressed Frames, 9, 96–97
    Marbled Shadowbox Frame, 107–10
    Spun Gold Mats, 98–99
    Tin Tile Frame, 100–1
Crazy Quilt Mat, 88–93
Cutting technique, 15
Cutting tools, 10

D
Decoupage Frame, 38–39
Dipping technique, 9, 98–99
Distressed Frames, 9, 96–97

F
Family treasures, framing, 37–53
    Burlap Mat, 51–53
    Chenille Script Mat, 44–45
    Decoupage Frame, 38–39
    Home Sweet Home Mat, 40–43
    Once Upon a Time Mat, 48–50
    Suitcase Frames, 46–47

Flowers, dried, 22–23, 51
Found object frames, 12
    Birthday Present, 29–31
    Crazy Quilt Mat, 88–93
    Penny Quilt Mat, 84–87
    Sweetheart, 20–21
    Tennis Racket, 72–73
    Tin Tile, 100–1
    Vintage Jewelry, 76–77
Frames
    assembly, 16–17
    boxes, 20–21, 29–31
    embellishments, 39
    nature adornments, 56–57
    ornament, 66–69
    patterned paper, 33–35
    selecting, 12
    See also Clay frames; Collections,
        framing; Family treasures,
        framing; Found object frames

G
Glass, 13
Gold paint dipping, 9, 98–99

H
Halloween frame, 24–25
Heritage photographs, 71–93
    Bead-Embellished Mat, 74–75
    Blended Clay Frame, 78–80
    Crazy Quilt Mat, 88–92
    Mosaic Clay Frame, 81–83
    Penny Quilt Mat, 84–87
    Tennis Racket Frame, 72–73
    Vintage Jewelry Frame, 76–77
Home Sweet Home Mat, 40–42

J
Jewelry, vintage, 76–77

K
Knives, 10

L
Leaf patterns, 64–69
Love in Bloom Mat, 22–23

M
Marbled Shadowbox Frame, 107–10
Mats
    bark and moss, 62–63
    beaded, 74–75, 111
    burlap, 51–53
    calligraphy on, 40–42, 44–45
    candy-covered, 24–25
    crazy quilt motif, 88–93
    cutting, 15
    dried botanicals on, 22–23, 51
    embossed tiles, 58–59
    leaf-stamped, 64–65
    vs. mounting, 14
    penny quilt motif, 84–87
    printed word motifs, 48–50
    seasonal patterns, 60–61
    spun gold, 98–99
    three-dimensional, 13

Memorabilia. *See* Collections, framing;
    Family treasures, framing
Mosaic Clay Frame, 81–83
Mosaic frames
    adhesive for, 11
    broken dishes, 102–3
    clay, 81–83
Mounting, 14

N
Nature motifs, 54–69
    Bark and Moss Frame, 62–63
    Sand and Shell Frame, 56–57
    Snowflake Mat, 60–61
    Stamped Leaf Mat, 64–65
    Sun Catcher Frame, 66–69
    Water Mat, 58–59
Needlework, stretching, 43

O
Once Upon a Time Mat, 48–50

P
Papers
    decorative patterns, 32–35
    marbled, 107–10
Patterns, enlarging and reducing, 17
Penny Quilt Mat, 84–87
Polymer clay. *See* Clay frames
Printed word motif, 48–50

Q
Quilt motifs
    crazy quilt, 88–93
    penny quilt, 84–87

S
Sand and Shell Frame, 56–57
Sealer, 10
Shadowbox frame, marbled, 107–10
Snowflake Mat, 60–61
Spun Gold Mats, 98–99
Stickers, 39
Suitcase Frames, 46–47
Sun Catcher Frame, 66–69
Supplies and equipment, 10–11
Sweetheart Frame, 20–21

T
Tennis Racket Frame, 72–73
Three-dimensional mats, glass with, 13
Tiles, embossed, 58–59
Tin Tile Frame, 100–101
Transfer paper, 17

V
Valentine's Day frame, 20–21
Varnish, 10
Vintage Jewelry Frame, 76–77

W
Water Mat, 58–59
Wedding frames, 20–23